The Christian Education of Youth

ULRICH ZWINGLI

GH
www.gideonhousebooks.com

The Christian Education of Youth

Ulrich Zwingli

© 2016 Gideon House Books

Published by:
Gideon House Books
2137 Ash Grove Way
Dallas, TX 75228
www.gideonhousebooks.com

Typesetting & Cover Design: Josh Pritchard

ISBN-13: 978-1-943133-32-1

Unless otherwise noted, Scripture quotations are from the Holy Bible, *New International Version*, © copyright 1973, 1978, 1984.

Contents

Preface

Ulrich Zwingli is well known as a reformer and theologian of the sixteenth century, but he is not so well known as an educator. Readers who have access to Zwingli's complete works and have time to collect from them what belongs to his educational career, will feel rewarded for the time spent in such work; but most persons interested in Zwingli have no time for research of this kind, and all such will be glad to read this little book.

As a matter of fact, the educational side of some religious leaders has not been presented in the history of education, fully enough to do them justice. The religious activity of these men involves an educational activity which, in many cases, is truly remarkable.

Several years ago, we read a reprint of Zwingli's educational treatise in the original dialect of Zurich. The peculiar charm of this dialect and the interest in the subject treated by Zwingli induced us to translate the treatise for our own satisfaction. Having been repeatedly advised to have this translation published, we finally proceeded to revise it for publication, and to write, also, as an introduction to it, a sketch of Zwingli's life from an educational point of view.

Zwingli first wrote his treatise in Latin and it was printed at Basel, in 1523, under the title, *"Quo pacto ingenui adolescentes informandi sint, Praeceptiones pauculae, Huldricho Zuinglio autore."* The Christian spirit of the treatise does not appear in this title, which means, *"In what manner noble youth ought to be instructed; a few precepts. Ulrich Zwingli, the author."* What the language of heathen Rome omitted in the title, Zwingli inserted, in preparing an edition, in the dialect of Zurich, for his Christian countrymen. It was printed in 1526, by Christoffel Froschauer, at Zurich, under the title, *"Wie man die Jugendt in guoten sitten und, Christenlicher zucht uferziehen unnd leeren soelle, ettliche kurtze underwysung, durch Huldrychen Zuinglin beschriben."* In English, this title reads thus: *"How one ought to bring up aud instruct youth in good manners and Christian discipline; a few short precepts, written by Ulrich Zwingli."* That he prepared this text himself for the printer, is the opinion of Director Israel, Zschopau, Saxony, and of Professor Staehelin, Basel, Switzerland. The latter is the latest standard authority on Zwingli's works, and the former selected this text, as the one from which to publish a reprint, for his collection of rare pedagogical works of the 16th and 17th centuries, rather than to follow the Latin edition of 1523 or the South German edition of 1524.

It is Director Isreal's reprint that we have translated into English, with little reference to any of the modern German texts on the life and works of Zwingli, in order to catch more fully, if possible, the spirit of Zwingli from the treatise, even if, occasionally, good English could have been much more easily written from the excellent modern German works.

In closing we may remark that Zwingli's treatise on the Christian Education of Youth was translated into English with title and date as follows: *"Certeyne Preceptes gathered by Hulricus Zwinglius declaring howe the ingenious Youth ought to be instructed and brought unto Christ. Ippeswich, 1548."* The present translation from the original, together with a sketch of the educational life of Zwingli, it is hoped, will add new interest to the study of Christian education in the Reformation period.

Alcide Reichenbach.
January, 1899.

A Sketch of Ulrich Zwingli's Life
as Related to Education

Switzerland, which is about one-third as large as the state of New York, has been the scene of many remarkable events in history. The ancients called the country Helvetia and the inhabitants were called Helvetii. They belonged to the Celtic race and were conquered by Marius and later, by Caesar. In the sixth century of our era the Franks subdued Helvetia, and from 1273 to 1291 Rudolph I., German Emperor, ruled over the territory, which was then called Higher Germany. August 1, 1291, ushered in the Swiss Confederation. All these are significant events, but the dawn of the Reformation in Switzerland overshadows them all, in far-reaching results. The Swiss Confederation has taught the world lessons of civil liberty; but the Reformation, begun so early in Switzerland, has taught the world lessons of religious liberty, which perpetuates civil liberty and frees the human spirit from the shackles of sin and death.

In the Providence of God, Ulrich Zwingli was called to be the pioneer and leader of the Reformation in Switzerland. He was the third son of his father, whose name was also Ulrich, and was born on New Year's Day, in the year 1484, near the mountain village Wildhaus, located in eastern Switzerland, near the source of the Thur, a tributary of the Rhine, and about twenty miles south of Lake Constance. If a traveler were to start at Basel and go a little south of east, in a straight line, for about forty-five miles, he would reach Zurich; and by continuing on the same line, about forty miles further, he would reach Wildhaus.

Young Ulrich inherited a strong constitution and an active, penetrating mind from his hardy and intelligent parents. His father, though a plain, simple mountaineer, had the honor of being elected magistrate of the parish. Ulrich learned many lessons from the book of nature, before he enjoyed the advantages of a school. The clear, bracing mountain air imparted vigor to his body and stimulated his mind to great activity. The majestic Alps, the beautiful pines, the tender grass, the lovely flowers, the wild animals, the grazing herds, and the yodel of the happy peasants taught him lessons of the true, the beautiful, and the good, which had their effect in molding his character and in shaping his career. The huge, solid rocks which the first confederates beheld on all sides, foreshadowed to them the stability of the confederacy; the Alpine peaks which surrounded Zwingli in his early youth, afterwards became to him the fingers of nature pointing to heaven, the sparkling springs were emblematic of the water of life, and the pure air was indicative of the pure Gospel truth freely offered to all mankind.

When Zwingli was eight years old, he was sent to his uncle, Bartholomew Zwingli, at Wesen, about twelve miles southwest of Wildhaus, in order to attend school. Having been instructed somewhat in the Scriptures by his grandmother and being eager to learn, young Ulrich made good use of his time in the primitive little school at Wesen. It may have been in his uncle's house, as many teachers of children in those days went from place to place, to teach in private houses. His uncle who was the village priest, no doubt did much to encourage him, and helped him in his studies.

The subjects studied in the elementary schools of that time were music, grammar, and probably writing. The grammar included some reading and orthography. Books were very scarce and not adapted to the wants of children, as printing had been introduced into Swiss towns only about fifteen years before this time. Most of the teaching was oral and very imperfect. The children had to repeat what the master told them and if they did not remember it, when it was again called for, they were often severely punished. Young Ulrich found it an easy matter to make rapid progress. Indeed, at the end of the second year, he had made so much progress, particularly in music, that his uncle thought it best to send him to a higher school, where he would have teachers who could teach him what he did not already know.

This picture of elementary schools, though gloomy, is much brighter than the one drawn by a good historian in referring to the educational status of the same canton two centuries prior to this time, when he says: "Of all the monks in the convent of St. Gall there was but one who could read and write."

In conversation with Ulrich's parents his uncle expressed a desire to have the boy sent to his friend, George Binzli, master of St. Theodore School, at Basel. This city had become a seat of learning through the founding of its University, in the year 1459. The existing schools were improved thereby and others were established. Ulrich could not go to the University, but he was well prepared to enter St. Theodore School. Accordingly, no time was lost, and Ulrich was sent to Basel in 1494, where he remained three years, studying Latin, music, and dialectics.

It was quite a trial for a lad of ten years to be sent to a school located down in the broad valley of the Rhine and so far from his elevated mountain home. The journey over the mountains and across the valleys seemed long, but it was nevertheless undertaken because Bartholomew Zwingli had full confidence in Binzli and believed that he would do justice to his nephew, in every study. Binzli took a special interest in his pupil from the beginning. Ulrich was studious, and the religious influence of his home as well as that of his uncle at Wesen, had already so fostered in him such a sense of duty that he soon adapted himself to the situation and entered with zeal upon the course of study in the new school. His talent for music was developed so rapidly that he delighted his companions and became a leader among them. In debate, which was a very popular exercise in the universities and which had even found its way into the schools, he soon exhibited wonderful power; and before the end of the third year, he became a peer to those who were older than he was. Master Binzli, though strongly attached to Ulrich, decided that another school should be selected for him. Having arrived at the age of thirteen years, Ulrich was able to pursue higher studies than those which he pursued in St. Theodore School.

After consultation with his parents, his uncle assisted young Zwingli to enter the school of Henry Woelflin, also called Lupulus, at Bern, which was fully as far from home as Basel. The latter city had few attractions for the young mountaineer, as it lies in an open plain, where the protection of rocky walls and high peaks was wanting; Bern presented the windings of the Aar to young Zwingli's eye, as Basel did the beautiful Rhine, and although built in a wide valley, the snow-capped mountains could be seen so well from Bern that he doubtless felt as though he were nearer home than at Basel.

Henry Woelflin was a learned man and had traveled in Palestine, Greece, and Rome. Thoroughly versed in the ancient classics and in history, and, withal, a poet of no mean rank, he was well prepared to found "the first academy of learned languages in Switzerland," or according to Myconius, the first Swiss humanistic institution.

Young Zwingli here found food for his vigorous mind and entered zealously upon the study of the Latin classics, in which he became so proficient that he tried to imitate the Latin poets. His poetical turn of mind was here brought to light and his skill in music became so great that he could play upon any instrument then in use. He sang well and exhibited wonderful powers of speech. He learned to speak Latin in a more finished style than that of his native Swiss dialect. Never afterwards did the love for classical literature grow cold in Zwingli's active life.

The Dominican monks, charmed by Zwingli's ability as a musician, tried to induce him to join their order. It seems that he wrote to his father, in regard to the matter, who at once called him home, in order to save him from the terrors of the monastery. Thus Zwingli studied at Bern, from 1497 to the latter part of the year 1499, preparing himself for entering a university.

According to the advice of his uncle, Zwingli was sent to the University of Vienna, where he was matriculated in the year 1500. The journey was at least four times as long as the one he had just made, but Zwingli was now sixteen years old and a long journey would be inspiring to him. The prospect of attending the University of Vienna, a flourishing institution having a history extending over a period of 135 years cheered his heart and made him feel that his desire for knowledge would be satisfied.

At this institution Zwingli was associated with students whose intellectual attainments were quite congenial to him. The names of some of them were afterwards recorded in history. One of his associates was later on known as Doctor Eck, the greatest Catholic theologian of Germany and a powerful opponent to Luther. Another bore the name of Glarean, from Glarus, his Swiss home; he afterwards became professor at the University of Basel and kept boarding students, among whom, in all probability, was Gerald Meyer, Zwingli's step-son. Zwingli, in the introduction to the little treatise on education dedicated to Gerald, speaks of the teacher of the latter as "our Glarean."

The studies which Zwingli pursued were mathematics, natural history, the Roman classics, poetry and music. He could build well on what he had learned under his great teacher Woelflin, at Bern. The father of Zwingli called him home in the year 1502, thus limiting his time at the University of Vienna to two years. The rich store of knowledge which Zwingli now possessed could not be utilized at Wildhaus, and, at the same time, his capacity and desire to learn were such that he could not stay at home; accordingly, he went back to Basel in the same year, but this time to be matriculated at the University. He had left Basel at the age of thirteen; he returned when he was eighteen years old. His age and scholarship now- fitted him to teach at St. Martin's School, while attending lectures in philosophy at the University.

He taught Latin with great success at St. Martin's School and his wonderful skill in music delighted his companions and set many of them to cultivating their talent for music. He studied the philosophy and the theology of his time more to refute the arguments of their expounders in later years than for any other purpose.

In the year 1505 the great theologian Wittenbach was called to Basel. He attacked the doctrines of the Roman Catholic Church and showed so clearly the rule of faith, by the word of God, that Zwingli, whose heart was prepared for the seed, became a disciple of Wittenbach and thus entered upon the study of theology in real earnest. He there laid the foundation for the great work of the Reformation, in which he played so active a part. Having rejected scholasticism, he turned to humanism for educational ideals and being convinced that error was demoralizing the Romish Church, he sought pure religious truth in the Bible.

In the year 1504, the University conferred upon Zwingli the degree of Bachelor of Arts. After two years of further study, he received the degree of Master of Arts, but he made no use of it and even said in regard to it, "One is our Master, even Christ."

His father and his uncle were relieved from contributing to his support during these four years spent at Basel, as Zwingli was enabled to support himself with the salary received at St. Martin's School.

Zwingli's student-life closed at institutions of learning, only to be continued to his death, in his profession as a minister of the Gospel. Before leaving Basel, he was called to the parish at Glarus, seven miles south of Wesen, where he had first attended school. How the young priest of twenty-two must have compared his last studies with his first, when he was a boy of eight years! He had grown very much more in mind than in body. He had been a student fourteen years, and quoting his words, "on no occasion has discipline been exercised upon me, yet I acknowledge that I am a great sinner before God." The American educator would sum up Zwingli's school-days thus : Two years in the primary school, at Wesen; three years in the grammar school, at Basel; three years in the academy, at Bern; four years of undergraduate study, two at the University of Vienna and two at the University of Basel; and two years of graduate study at the latter University.

Zwingli gave time enough to higher education to become a good scholar; but his educational career had, in a certain sense, only begun. At Glarus, in addition to the duties which he performed as pastor, he founded a Latin School, which he conducted with signal success. His younger brother James was one of his pupils. Some of those who made the most progress he sent to Vienna, others to Basel.

The study of the Roman classics was continued, with all the work that he did as pastor and master of a school. Cicero, Caesar, Sallust, Livy, Suetonius, Pliny, Seneca, and Tacitus were his Roman companions and the critical study of their thoughts was his delight. He took much pains to become a good public speaker and studied for this purpose the masterpieces of eloquence. He once said: "A man must know two things above all others, namely, God and how to speak."

More than all else he studied the Bible to find therein the rule of life, so that he might the more faithfully carry out the resolution he had made when he came to Glarus, namely, "I shall be true and upright towards God and man in every circumstance of life into which the hand of the Lord may place me."

Glarus, the place where, it is said, slates were first used in a school, was never forgotten by a few Swiss scholars who studied in Zwingli's Latin School. He had introduced into his school the modern notion of sympathy between teacher and pupil, and his pupils became quite proficient in the Latin classics. Such a school deserves a paragraph in the history of education. Aegidius Tschudi, who afterwards made his mark as a Swiss historian, wrote to Zwingli from Basel: "Help me that I may be recalled to you, for with no one would I desire so much to live as with you." Valentine Tschudi, a cousin of Aegidius, wrote: "How could I ever cease thanking you for your great kindness! As often as I returned home, and in a special manner quite recently when I lay sick of a fever for four days, also when I forgot my books at Basel, you invited me to come to you, but I feared in my timidity, that I might become a burden to you; and you encouraged me, offered me your books, your help and services. To me, also, your benevolence to all students overflowed, and that, too, not in a general way, but with studious regard to my circumstances and necessities your treasures of learning were at my disposal."

We are not told how long this Latin School was under Zwingli's direction. Several times during his ten years of service at Glarus, he was called away long enough to close the Latin School or to place it in the hands of other persons. We do know, however, that he was not satisfied with all the research that he made in the Roman classics; for in the year 1513, he began the study of Greek without the aid of a teacher. He succeeded so well that he could soon read Greek authors with ease. He once remarked that Greek had become as easy for him as conversing with a friend. In the course of time he read Hesiod, Homer, Pindar, Thucydides, Demosthenes, Plato, and

Aristotle. In later years he also wrote explanatory notes on Homer and Pindar. The latter seems to have been one of his favorite authors. "According to my conviction," said he, "no other Greek writer serves so valuable a purpose to throw light upon the Holy Scriptures as this one. Antiquity, as every other period, has peculiarities which can only be understood, by familiar intercourse with the ancients themselves. Pindar resembles that sacred period, not only in his language but also in the direction of his thought and in his inmost being." Above all else, he desired to read the New Testament in Greek, in order to obtain better and clearer views of the truth. He even copied all the epistles of St. Paul in Greek, in order that he might carry them with him and commit them to memory. In the same manner, he afterwards copied other portions of the Bible.

Before leaving Giants, Zwingli became intensely interested in reforms, in matters of religion. In the year 1514, he met the learned Erasmus, the humble Myconius, and the eloquent Oecolampadius, at Basel. The light thrown upon reforms in religion by these men so filled Zwingli's mind with zeal for the truth that his students and his friends at home were delighted with his preaching.

In the year 1516, this wonderful student of Bible truth and classic writers was called to Einsiedeln, about sixteen miles to the northwest, Valentine Tschudi, his former pupil in the Latin School, becoming his successor to Glarus. Zwingli had now become an attractive and eloquent speaker, as well as a finished scholar and zealous reformer. The superstitious practices at Einsiedeln furnished him an opportunity to make use of his wonderful talents. He fearlessly attacked the advocates of Romish errors and preached reform to large and attentive audiences. Perhaps no other man could have so impressed his hearers as to cause nuns to return to their parents and pilgrims to turn away from the sacred shrine in despair, or to Jesus as their only Savior. Two years seemed to suffice to prepare Zwingli for a new field of activity, to which we must follow him in order to complete his remarkable educational career.

Called to Zurich, in the year 1518, Zwingli was better prepared than ever before to expose the errors of Rome. Having begun in the year 1516 to preach the pure Gospel, he had now become a powerful exponent of the truth as it is in Christ Jesus, and his persevering study of oratory gave his cheerful manner and his convincing arguments an attractiveness that drew crowds to hear his sermons, which, during the first four years of his pastorate at Zurich, covered the subject matter of seven books in the New Testament. The Reformation was progressing rapidly at Zurich.

During this time Zwingli began the study of Hebrew under the direction of Andrew Boeschenstein, who had come to Zurich and offered to teach Hebrew to any who wished to study it. In the fifth year of Zwingli's pastorate at Zurich, he explained the value of the Hebrew language to every student of the Bible, in his short treatise on Christian education. No one was more faithful in the study of Hebrew and no one made more progress than Zwingli; the linguistic power which he already possessed enabled him to overcome the difficulties of the Hebrew language and to discover its genius, in a remarkably short time. He soon read the Old Testament with great satisfaction, because the Hebrew text conveyed to his mind clearer notions of the truth. Zwingli's wonderful perseverance in the study of languages, at a time when he might have been content with the meagre attainments of most parish priests, ought to awaken admiration for him in the mind of every student of to-day, and should make him zealous to excel in linguistic study, according to the demands of the present age.

In order to understand how it came about that Zwingli wrote on Christian education, it becomes necessary to refer to his social life at Zurich, and to the habits of the youth at that time.

Anna Reinhardt, a plain and unassuming girl, yet talented, amiable, and spotless in character was married, in 1504, to John Meyer von Knonau, a nobleman near Zurich. His father was so displeased with him for having been unwilling to marry a maiden selected for him from the ranks of the nobility that he would have nothing whatever to do with John and his amiable wife. In the course of time John Meyer enlisted in the Italian military service, as many other Swiss did at that time, and in 1517 he died. The sad widow felt that she was forsaken with her little son Gerald, who was then eight years old, and her two daughters younger than he. She lived in the town of Zurich, making her living as well as she could. One day she went to market, where her father-in-law Meyer saw little Gerald playing about the market. He was struck with the appearance of the little boy and after inquiring who the handsome little fellow was, Mr. Meyer was told that the boy was his grandchild. This touched the old man's heart and he at once received the lonely widow Anna as a member of his family.

In the year 1518, Mr. Meyer died, but it seems that he had provided for Anna in such a way that she was comfortably situated in her own house, and her children, as Zwingli afterwards once said, "had wealth enough." Anna

Meyer now lived for her children, leading them in the path of virtue and providing for their education.

At about the same time when Anna Meyer lost her father-in-law, Zwingli came to Zurich and he happened to reside in a house adjoining Anna Meyer's home. She became one of the first and most attentive listeners to his preaching. Her beautiful character must have made a good impression upon his mind, from the beginning. Her devotion to the proper training of her children must have led Zwingli to see in her a model mother. Gerald once came to Zwingli's house, on an errand. The conversation which followed caused Zwingli to admire the boy and to help him, later, in his studies. In 1521, when Gerald was twelve years old, Zwingli sent him to Basel, where he was at first taught by Jacob Nepos and afterwards by Glarean, Zwingli's friend. Gerald learned Latin so well that in the same year, he wrote Zwingli a letter in Latin that would be equal to twenty-five lines of the average text on Cicero's orations.

Although Gerald seemed to have inherited something of his father's wild disposition and did not always escape discipline, he still treasured up the religious truth received from his mother and from Zwingli, thereby laying the foundation for that noble manhood which prompted him to remain true to God and his country, till he fell with Zwingli on the field of battle.

Early in 1522, Anna Meyer was married to Zwingli, privately, according to a custom then coming into vogue among the clergy, in order not to excite the wrath of the enemies of the Reformation. She was then thirty-seven years old, a year younger than Zwingli. Zurich was soon prepared for public marriage of the clergy, however; so that on the second of April, 1524, Zwingli's marriage was celebrated, publicly, to the joy of his numerous friends. The following year, Zurich actually passed laws relating to marriage, conformably to Zwingli's private and public marriage.

Gerald Meyer, having returned from Basel, after two years of study, now met Zwingli, not only as a father in the faith but as his father by marriage. The bonds of attachment thus formed induced Zwingli all the more to have Gerald's highest welfare at heart. During the summer of 1523 Gerald, then a lad of fourteen, spent some time at the hot baths in the mountains and returned to Zurich before Zwingli had time to get a present ready for him, according to the custom at that time.

Zwingli, to protect the sprightly Gerald from the pernicious influence of reckless companions and to reform the training of youth and the conduct of the young in society, had planned a treatise on Christian education, some time prior to this, but he had failed to find time to write it. The return from the bath furnished an occasion which Zwingli could not pass by unimproved; consequently, he took the time to write in Latin, for the young student of the classics, the instructive and edifying treatise on Christian education and dedicated it to him, on the first day of August.

This short treatise exhibits, in a remarkable degree, Zwingli's keen insight into the intellectual, moral, and religious needs of youth. Though short, it was worth more to Gerald than a present of gold and precious stones, because its influence upon his character could not fail to be lasting. Zwingli clearly marked out the way in which Gerald should walk and how he should prepare to walk therein. He laid down as much of science and art, in his course, as the teachers in those days could teach, and the study of religion and morals was emphasized in keeping with the evangelical spirit of the great reformer. The culture which Gerald was to receive from following Zwingli's teaching reached out into nearly all the avenues of life. Although no principles of education are categorically laid down, the treatise breathes them throughout, in the study and practice recommended.

The Rev. K. Fulda, editor of the reprint of the South-German edition of 1524, declares the latter to be the *first* Protestant treatise on pedagogy. He makes no mention of the Latin edition of 1523, which is still earlier and therefore in no sense an imitation, but an original protestant production. Truly, this modest treatise, to which an otherwise excellent French history of pedagogy makes a one-sided reference, by mentioning only certain elements of secular education contained therein, deserves a place of high honor in Christian pedagogical literature.

In support of this opinion, we quote from Moerikofer: "It is too serious and thoughtful a production to be regarded only as a friendly message on a social occasion Zwingli knew well that the wild disposition of the Swiss youth was fostered by the corrupt civil life of that time and that through love of close application to study, honest labor, and noble aspirations a better time must come. Scarcely was any other man so well prepared as he to work for this end; hence, Christian earnestness, humanistic wisdom, and training for contact with the world are united in a beautiful, harmonious whole ...It is a safe philosophy of life, emanating from a thoroughly trained and experienced man, whose heart was filled with the abiding joys of a higher life in the light of the Holy Gospel." No one will thus appreciate the reading of the treatise, however, who does not fully imagine himself carried back to Zwingli's time, so as to see, mentally, the crude, unscientific methods of pedagogy, fettered by the shackles of scholasticism. Then, too, Zwingli's style is often loose and sometimes lacks method; he wrote in too many languages, and he was too busily engaged to rewrite or even review what he had hastily written. Zwingli never wrote books for pecuniary gain, *for he never accepted money to write a book.*

Head-master Niessli of the Carolinum, named after Charles the Great, who had granted letters for an ecclesiastical foundation, at Zurich, was removed by death and Zwingli was elected as his successor, April 14, 1525. This institution had declined as a gymnasium, with the churches of the city, on account of the idleness and corruption of the religious and educational leaders; hence Zwingli sought to reform the Carolinum as well as the churches, as a necessary part of the great work of the Reformation.[1]

Accordingly, on the 19th of June, in the same year, he substituted for the choir-service what he called "prophecy," according to 1 Cor. 14, thus engrafting upon the Carolinum a higher institution which transformed it into a remarkably practical school of theology, ancient languages, and elementary science. It is here that Zwingli accomplished his greatest work, as an educator. The school was in session every weekday, Friday excepted, and was opened at 7 o'clock in the morning, in the summer, and at 8 o'clock, in the winter. A month's vacation was granted three times a year. The course of study centered on the Bible. The first hour, i. e. the "prophecy" proper, was given to exegesis, with some elements of systematic and practical theology to meet the wants of the Reformation. The second hour consisted of a divine service, in which the people of the city took part with the students, among whom were also town-parsons, predicants, canons, and chaplains. Here the same Scriptures were treated again, but so simplified that the people could understand them; and we may add that the students themselves not only obtained a clearer knowledge from this repetition but they also learned, in a most practical manner, how to present the truth in their future charges. Friday was market-day, and the people from the country came to hear the preaching, which was largely intended for their special benefit. The afternoon of each school-day was devoted to the study of the languages and elementary science.

The first professor chosen to assist Zwingli was Ceporin, a Greek and Hebrew scholar of great merit. He was elected, June 5, 1525, but he had been teaching at Zurich, in 1522, and later, at Basel, where his Greek grammar was printed. At the Carolinum, he filled the chair of professor of Hebrew, but only till December 20th of the same year, when he died from over-exertion, at the age of 26. In March, the following spring, the learned Pellican became his successor. Jacob Ammann was, at the same time, elected professor of Latin and Rudolph Collin, professor of Greek. Megander, Leo Jud, and Myconius also assisted Zwingli. Myconius, however, taught at the Frauenminster School, but he conducted an exercise in New Testament exegesis there, every afternoon at three o'clock, which crowds of the laity and students attended, whereas Zwingli had charge of Old Testament exegesis, at the Carolinum, besides being its head and also the pastor of a congregation.

The call of Pellican includes the salary to be paid him, which was to be equal to Zwingli's, namely, sixty to seventy florins and lodging.

The "prophecy," or theological department proper, was conducted as follows: Zwingli offered a prayer to the effect that God might enlighten every mind and make each one to understand rightly his Word. Then followed the reading of a portion of Scripture from the Vulgate, by a scholar, with comments by Megander; the same verses were then read in Hebrew and explained critically, doctrinally, and practically, in Latin, by Pellican; thereafter, Zwingli compared both texts with the Septuagint and further explained and applied the text, practically; finally, Leo Jud turned the last text and its applications into good German. If something better was revealed to anyone else, the speaker gave him the privilege of making it known.

The languages seem to have been taught by memorizing and constant speaking. A student present, in August, says: "At six o'clock in the morning, the first book of Virgil's Aeneid is read. All those verses of Virgil must be memorized. The second lesson is on Cicero's letters to his friends, the best of which must also be memorized. These are the morning lessons. Then we read Homer, compose letters, and write a poem."

If one could see all the obstacles put in Zwingli's way, as well as the natural circumstances of his time, the establishment of this wonderful school of theology would appear all the more astonishing. Most men would have been content with zealous preaching, but Zwingli's activity extended even beyond the limits of teaching and preaching. He also wrote a number of books, carried on an extensive correspondence, and defended the cause of reform in public debate. In 1528, it required discussions lasting nineteen days, at Bern, to establish the Reformation there.

It is impossible to understand how Zwingli could do all these things, and do them so well, until we know the secret of his success. Zwingli had exceptional intellectual ability and worked speedily, systematically, and incessantly; besides all this, he possessed herculean powers of endurance.

On one occasion, he aided the reformers in their debate, at Baden, fourteen miles northwest of Zurich, by sending messengers, every night, with letters expressing his views; and so busily was he then engaged, that he did not go to bed at all, for six weeks. His iron constitution and his quick, penetrating intellect enabled him to accomplish a work that is grander and more enduring than the much admired snow-capped Alps that pierce the clouds and tower up into the clear, blue sky. As early as 1514, Erasmus said that he expected Zwingli to raise his country to a higher plane of learning and morals, along with like-minded men of other nations. How much higher he could have raised it, had he not been cut down, in the midst of his labors, October n, 1531, on the cruel battle-field of Cappel!

> The hero died and all reformers wept,
>> The loss to them was great and fierce the strife;
> But greater was the gain to him that slept,
>> For he had gone to reap eternal life.

How One Ought To Bring Up And Instruct Youth In Good Manners And Christian Discipline; A Few Short Precepts, By Ulrich Zwingli

Grace and peace from God and our Lord Jesus Christ be unto the honorable and discreet youth, Gerald Meyer, by Ulrich Zwingli.

As you have just returned from the bath and as everyone else has received you with gladness, some presenting you with one gift and others with another, I thought it would be unkind and even rude on my part, my dear Gerald, were I not also to receive you with a present provided for you. I feel all the more pressed to do this, because it is the general custom among good friends thus to honor those returning from health resorts or even before they return.

I have a twofold reason for counting you among my dear friends. You earnestly devote yourself to art and learning, and I hope not without good results. You also strive diligently after learning in the ranks of the young heroes, in the school of our Glarean, the learned and well-informed instructor and master.

In thinking much, for a long time, about what would be most agreeable to you, I have come to the conclusion that the present, in order to please you, should be of a sacred character or of the character of the liberal arts, or it should partake of the nature of both. As you are inclined to godliness and virtue, you also manifest, at an early age, the agreeable fruits of good citizenship and nobleness of character. Though I diligently sought to give you something pertaining to the arts but failed to succeed, I thought it not without value to you and perhaps I might render you a lasting service, if I were to instruct you in certain things pertaining not only to the health of the body but also to the good of the soul. Remembering that I had planned, some time ago, to write a little book on the manner of instructing and training youth, and that I was prevented from carrying out what I had in mind, by many untoward circumstances, as you can now see, it occurred to me, in thinking about a present for you, that my former intention should now be carried out.

Although I see some who are exceedingly careful to place a perfect work of art into the hands of one really worthy of it, I find myself defeated at this point; for the one to whom I desire to dedicate such a work is already present, and I have not the leisure of an artist, nor the nine years of time afterwards to store up the masterpiece [Horace De Arte Poetica, V., 386 et seq.]. Being now in a dilemma, since, on the one hand, I ought to make you a present, and on the other, I have no time to prepare anything without haste and according to the custom, I have found a way, as I believe, that will satisfy both of us on this occasion. I have robbed my occupation of so much time as to collect hastily, certain instructions; but they will be brief and carefully considered, lest you should become weary of reading to the end. As a rule, when little of a good thing is given, more is wanted.

What I teach you here, I hope you will not judge from its style; but I trust that you will appreciate it, on account of its significance and because it comes from the heart. He who is not godless may promise to [write about] holy things [in so short a time], but the most learned man would be ashamed to promise a finished work.

My subject will be treated under three heads: Part first tells how the delicate mind of youth should be nurtured and instructed in the things pertaining to God; part second instructs the youth in the things pertaining to himself; and part third shows how a youth should act towards other persons.

In this undertaking I do not have in view the instruction of infants, nor the manner in which pupils should be taught, when they begin to go to school; but the instruction and conduct of those who have arrived at an age in which they are clever and intelligent and, as men say, are able to swim without dry bark.

I regard you as now having arrived at this age. It is to be hoped that you will read these thoughts attentively and frequently, and that you will conform your life to them, in order that other youths may learn of you as a living example. May God work out these things in your heart. Amen.

Given at Zurich, on the first day of August, in the year 1523.

PART I

How The Delicate Mind Of Youth Should Be Nurtured And Instructed In The Things Pertaining To God

First of all, let me say that, although man can in no wise draw his own heart to faith in the only true God, even if one could surpass in power of speech the celebrated and eloquent Pericles, but only our heavenly Father who draws us to Himself can do these things; yet faith comes, according to the apostle Paul, by hearing, in so far as such hearing is the hearing of the Word of God. Do not understand, however, that the preaching of the mere spoken Word can accomplish so much, unless the Spirit within attracts and speaks. For this reason, must faith be implanted in the heart of a youth with pure and sacred words coming, as it were, from God himself. The speaker should, at the same time, also pray to Him who alone can work faith, to the end that He may enlighten by his Spirit, the one who is being instructed in the Word of God.

To my mind, it does not seem inconsistent with the teachings of Christ to lead the young to a knowledge of God through sensible objects. When the beautiful structure of the whole world is placed before their eyes, each created object points, as with a finger, to the mutability and the destructibility of all existing things; whereas he who so firmly established and harmoniously united these numberless things must be eternal and immutable. To this it should be added that he who so wisely and skillfully arranged all things ought, in no wise, to be mistrusted or supposed to forget his works or to fail to guide them all in harmony; for among men, a father would be regarded as wicked, if he did not diligently care for his household.

From this the youth will learn that the providence of God provides all things, orders all things, upholds all things; for, of two sparrows bought for a farthing, one does not fall to the ground without the providence of God, who has numbered the very hairs of our heads. His care and watchfulness surely do not diminish when the object for which God cares is small or insignificant.

It is clear from these considerations, that God, in his providence, foreordains and provides not only the things for the soul but also those needed for the body; hence, also, we see how He feeds the ravens and how beautifully He clothes and adorns the lilies of the field. Where the human mind is rightly imbued with the teaching of the providence of God, there it can no longer be anxious about food and clothing, much less be shamefully avaricious. The mind will be kept from a dangerous poison, if the temptation to avarice and the worry about making one's living be cut off and uprooted, as soon as they appear. The mind will then know that God is not only Lord, but also the Father of all those who trust in Him,—that He would have us go to Him for help no less than we go to our earthly father, and that He promised help in his own words, yea, invites us to come to Him in prayer.

When we are attacked by disease, therefore, whether it be of the soul or of the body, we are taught to pray to God alone for the true remedy. When the enemy oppresses us and with envy and hatred makes our burden heavy, we are to flee to Him alone. When we desire knowledge or skill or wisdom, we know that we are to ask these things of God. Even wife and children are to be asked of Him. When riches and honor are bestowed upon us more freely than upon others, we ought to pray to God that our hearts may not grow faint and that we be not led astray.

What more need I say? If our minds be so informed as I said before, we shall feel that all things are to be sought from God. We shall also regard it an offense against God to ask of Him favors which should not be bestowed upon us; yea, we shall be ashamed to desire or to possess anything unbecoming to us in the sight of God; on the contrary, we will strive only after those things which are enduring and will further our salvation.

The youth whom we have before us for instruction will come to a knowledge of the mysteries of the Gospel in the following manner: In the first place, he must learn about the condition of our first parents, how they died after they had transgressed the command of God. Then, he must learn how they, with their sins, brought the whole human race under sin and condemnation ; for the dead cannot give birth to living beings, no more than Moors are ever seen to be born of British parents. From all this our youth will come to know his own infirmities and his sin-sick condition. These infirmities he will also feel, when he knows that we do all things in weakness, or through frailty, or from selfish motives, or through temptation; and when he knows, too, that God is infinitely far from temptation, since there can be no temptation or weakness in Him. It undoubtedly follows from this that we, if we desire to dwell with God [in heaven], must become free from temptation. Just as the righteous man will have no association with the wicked man and as the wicked man also cannot bear the conduct of the righteous; so, also, no one shall dwell with God, except he only who is without spot or blemish, being pure in heart and holy, even as God is holy; for "blessed are the pure in heart, for they shall see God."

Such a state of innocence and holiness we shall not be able to attain, as long as we are surrounded, on all sides, by temptations. Here we are in a sad dilemma. As God requires such a state of innocence, purity, and holiness and yet, as we are unable of ourselves to do anything but evil in His sight, being poisoned by sin and full of vice, we have no other way but to surrender ourselves to God and to look to Him for mercy.

Then will dawn upon us the light of the Gospel, the glorious news made known to us, namely, that from such anxiety and misery, from such wretchedness, in which we all lie bound, Christ redeems us; for He is such a Savior, Restorer, and Preserver that the greatest heathen god can in no way be likened unto Him. This Jesus gives peace to our consciences, which hitherto caused us to be in despair; yea, He draws us to Himself that we may implicitly trust in Him and thus are we saved. Since He is entirely free from all infirmities and temptations, for He was conceived by the Holy Ghost and born of a pure and innocent virgin, He first offered up his innocence and righteousness in our stead; and having borne our burdens, pains, and diseases He thereby saved all those that firmly believe these things. For whoever accepts by faith this free gift, which is offered to the lost human race by God through Christ, is saved and henceforth becomes a joint heir with Christ; wherefore he also will be with the Father in eternal bliss, for He wills that his servants be where He is.

The innocence, purity, and righteousness of Christ, which He offered up for our guilt and condemnation, deliver us from sin, guilt, and suffering; and we are reckoned worthy of the favor of God, for the reason that Christ, who was absolutely free from all sinful inclination, was able to satisfy fully the justice of God. Although He is so high and holy, namely, very God, He nevertheless is our Savior. From this it follows that his righteousness and innocence, which are wanting in us, are also imputed to us; for God made Him unto us wisdom, righteousness, sanctification and redemption. So we now have access to God through Christ, because He is our Savior and a pledge of the grace of God unto us. He is our surety, our bondsman, our mediator, our advocate, and our intercessor; yea, He is a perfect Savior to us.

Those who have thus received the Gospel and assuredly trust therein are born of God; for the shortsightedness of the human mind can neither perceive nor understand the heavenly and mysterious council of God's grace.

This truth accounts for the fact that those who are born again through the Gospel do not sin; for he that is born of God doth not commit sin. Whoever believes in the Gospel is born of God. So, then, do those not sin who are born again through the Gospel. To explain more fully, it will suffice to say that their sins are not reckoned to them unto death and damnation, because Christ has paid the debt and has washed away their sins, by having become a precious ransom through his death on the cross.

Although we, while we are in this mortal body and are justly removed far from the Lord in our misery, are unable to escape from temptation and are therefore not without sin; yet Christ, because He is our Savior, makes full amends for our weakness and failings. As He is an everlasting, an eternal Spirit, He is also so dear and precious in the sight of God, that He pays our debt and takes away our sins; yea, Christ's merits far surpass our sins and transgressions.

Such assured confidence in Christ, however, does not make men lazy, does not make them negligent nor careless; but on the contrary, it awakens us, urges us on, and makes us active in doing good and living righteous lives, since such assured confidence cannot come from man. How could it be that the human mind, which is given almost wholly to impressions from without, would lean entirely, and in all hopefulness and confidence, upon a thing which is invisible and which can in no wise be perceived by the senses? From this it is to be understood that this faith and assured confidence in Christ must come from God only. Now, where God works, you need not fear that the cause will not prosper or that good deeds will not follow.

Inasmuch as God is a perfect, everlasting being, and a moving power which is immovable, but which moves all things else, He will ever move and actively engage those whose hearts He has drawn to Himself. This opinion does not require proof, but practice and experience. Only the believers in

Christ learn and experience how He engages them in his service and with how much courage and joy they continue in the work of the Lord.

Now he who has well learned the mysteries of the Gospel and rightly understands them will endeavor to live a righteous life; therefore the Gospel should be taught most diligently and, as much as may be, in all its purity. We should also very early teach the young how to practice those things which please God most, those,—in fact, which He continually is to us, namely, truth, justice, mercy, faithfulness, and righteousness. For if God be a Spirit, He can be rightly honored with no other offering than a submissive mind. Therefore every youth should see to it, in all diligence, that he strive early to walk in the way that will make him become a pious man, and that, as much as in him lies, his life be innocent and godlike. The Lord does good to all men; He is helpful to everyone and wounds no person, unless he be one who has already done harm to himself. So, also, he who endeavors to be useful to all men and tries to be all things to all men, and who keeps his heart free from all iniquity, comes nearest to the likeness of God. These things are of an exalted character and difficult to do, if we look to our own strength; but to him that believeth, all things are possible.

PART II

Those Things That Pertain
To The Youth Himself

I.

Now, after the youthful mind, which is to be established in virtue, has been rightly molded through faith, the youth should, in consequence of this, order well and adorn beautifully his own heart. Then, after he is rightly and well-ordered within himself, he can also advise and assist other persons.

He cannot order his mind and prepare his heart better, however, than by engaging in the study of the Word of God, day and night. This he can do more skillfully and advantageously, when he thoroughly understands Hebrew and Greek; for he will succeed very poorly in gaining a clear and exact knowledge of the Old Testament, without the aid of the former, and of the New Testament, without the aid of the latter.

While we are instructing those who are well grounded in the elements of knowledge, I do not deem it proper to omit the study of the Latin language altogether, as this language is now being so generally used. Although it is less helpful to a clear understanding of the Holy Scriptures than the Greek or the Hebrew language, it is none the less useful for other purposes in active life. It often happens, too, that we come in contact with Latin scholars, in carrying on the work of the Lord Jesus Christ. Far be it from a Christian, however, to use the languages for mere pecuniary gain or pleasure; for they are a gift of the Holy Ghost.

The next language after the Latin, which we should endeavor to study, is the Greek. We should study it, as already stated, for reading the New Testament in the original; for I take the liberty to say that, as I understand the matter, it seems to me that the doctrines of Christ were not treated so carefully nor taught so purely from the beginning, by the Latin scholars, as they were, by the Greek scholars. For this reason, let the youth be led to the original Gospel language.

The student of the Latin and Greek languages must see to it that he keep his heart in faith and innocence; for there are many things in these languages that have been studied to the detriment of the student, among which are wantonness, craftiness, a domineering and warlike spirit, useless and vain philosophy, and the like. If the mind be warned in due time, it can, like Ulysses, pass by these evils, untouched and unharmed. This will be the case; if the student, at the first warning of his conscience, says to himself: This you hear in order that you should take warning and flee from it, and not that you should accept it.

The Hebrew language I place last, because the use of the Latin is so general and the Greek naturally follows the Latin; otherwise I should have given the Hebrew the first place, and justly, too, because anyone who does not know the properties and the peculiarities of this language will find it a difficult task, in many passages, even among Greek scholars, to discover the real sense and natural meaning of the Scriptures. The object I have in view, however, is not to speak at great length of the languages.

With such preparation must he be equipped who would arrive at the inner meaning of this heavenly wisdom, to which no other can be compared, much less made equal. Let him, however, approach it in a humble spirit and thirsting after righteousness.

After he has penetrated thus far into the hidden things of God, he will find many examples to show him how to live righteously, first among which is Christ who is the complete and perfect pattern of all virtues. If he comes to know Christ fully, from the words and the works of the latter, he will so accept Him that in all his works, councils, and business relations he will endeavor to give proof of Christ's virtues, as far as it is possible for man in his weakness and frailty to do.

He will learn from Christ when to speak and when to be silent, each in its own time. He will be ashamed to speak, in his early youth, of those things which belong only to the conversation of men, when he learns that Christ did not begin to speak in public till he was thirty years old; therefore long after he had given proof of his mission, before the doctors in his twelfth year. Hence, rather than to put himself forward when he is very young, the youth will early seek to understand great things that are pleasing to God.

Now, just as the greatest ornament to a woman is to be silent, so, also, nothing is more becoming to a youth than to try faithfully to be silent for a certain time, until not only the understanding but also the tongue, each for itself and both together, are trained and work harmoniously together. I do not mean that youths shall be silent five years, as Pythagoras commanded his pupils; but I would restrain them from being too eager and hasty to speak, and unless it be to speak about useful or necessary matters, they should not speak at all.

If a youth is learning the art of expression from his teacher and if the latter has any defect or any disagreeableness in his speech, the youth should not imitate these unpleasant things in his teacher's speech. This hint is by no means to be regarded as being of little account; for we learn from the writings of the ancients that some imitated their masters not only in errors of speech, but also in the awkward movements of the body.

Any person can easily recognize slowness of speech or a stammering tongue; but I want to call attention to the fact that errors are made in the enunciation of words and in the tones of the voice, not mentioning the artistic qualities of the latter, as this is not the place to speak of them. These errors are made, when the speaker speaks too rapidly or too slowly, when his voice lacks force and its pitch is too low, when its force is too great and its pitch is too high, and when any speech whatsoever is delivered in a monotone and the visible expression is unchanged or otherwise not in accordance with the subject-matter of the speech. It has been observed that elephants, when they are by themselves, practice those things diligently, which they had failed to do before and had suffered punishment on that account. So, also, should every youth see to it that he practices diligently and at frequent intervals, in chaste facial expression, and in gestures which are so graceful that he will never clumsily swing his arms as if he were rowing.

These things he should regulate in such a manner that they serve the cause of truth instead of flattering his hearers; for how can a Christian heart endure the lascivious manners of some persons? I have no other object in view, when I want a youth to refine his manners, than that every one may be led thereby to free himself from external rudeness or unbecoming manners; because these are not uncertain signs of uncouthness or coarseness of character.

Above all things the mind must be firm in the truth and unmoved by evil influences. If this be the case, it can easily overcome the wild or awkward movements of the body. For example, let the youth refrain from wrinkling his forehead, or making a wry face, or twisting his mouth, or shaking his head, or swinging his hands to and fro. On the other hand, let all his movements be so under control as to indicate plainness, simplicity, and graceful modesty. Let this suffice in regard to speaking and remaining silent.

Arithmetic, surveying, and music, I think, no youth should neglect; but he should not spend too much time on these studies. Although they are very valuable to everyone who is skillful in their application and although he who never studies them suffers much from his ignorance, yet no one should become old in studying them; for if he does, he will not derive more benefit from them than does the man who walks back and forth simply to avoid being idle.

II.

Let every youth flee from intemperance as he would from a poison; for, in addition to the fact that it makes furious the body, which is of itself inclined to vehemence, it brings on premature old age; because the body becomes disordered from the beginning. From this it follows that, if the intemperate man becomes old at all and believes that he will find rest in his latter days, he will be deceived and will find nothing but disease. For it cannot be that he who has habituated himself to revel in wine does not, in the end, suffer from dangerous diseases. I refer to epilepsy, paralysis, dropsy, leprosy, and the like. So, then, if you desire to be old a long time, become old [wise] early.

One's food should be plain and simple; for why should a youth, whose stomach is strong and always ready for digestion, need to eat partridges, fieldfares, woodcocks, capons, venison, and like delicacies? Let him rather put off eating these things until he is old, when his teeth will be worn down, his palate and throat hardened from long use, his stomach weakened, and his body deprived of its vigor. Then he will need such food. How can one attain to old age and sustain his strength during the same, if, as a high-spirited youth, one gives himself up to indulgence in those things which old men need for bodily sustenance and enjoyment?

Hunger should simply be satisfied by eating, not driven away never to return. It is related of Galenus that he lived a hundred and twenty years, because he had never left the table, with his hunger satisfied. I do not mean to say that you shall starve yourself, but that you shall not become a slave to beastly appetite, against which life demands that you should struggle. I know very well that men sin by going to either extreme, namely, by becoming like wolves in ravenous appetite or by becoming unfit for work on account of being half starved.[3]

Nothing seems to me to be more foolish than to seek honor and praise, by wearing costly clothing. From such a point of view, the pope's asses could be respected and highly honored; for if they are strong animals, they can carry more gold, silver, and precious stones than the strongest man. Who would not be ashamed of parading his costly clothing, when he hears that the Son of God and of the Virgin Mary cried in the manger, not having more swaddling-clothes around Him than the Virgin Mary carried with her, as she was not prepared for a birth in such a place.

Those who put on strange or new clothing every day thereby show how fickle, or at least how effeminate and childish they are. Such persons do not belong to Christ. While they thus clothe themselves in rare attire, they let the poor suffer from cold and hunger. For this reason a Christian should beware of foolishness and extravagance in dress, as well as of any other evil.

When a youth begins to be fond of young ladies and falls in love with them, he should show how gallant and strong minded he is. Just as daring young knights test their strength and their arms in war, so it behooves the Christian youth to exert all his powers to overcome every temptation to foolish and unlawful love. If he nevertheless seeks the company of young ladies, let him beware of inordinate affection; and he should select the company of one whose manners and conduct he would be willing to endure through the varied scenes of wedlock. Let him pay attention to her, but his affectionate relation to her, as one chosen for marriage, must be pure and so true that, among all women, he will love no other.

Why need I forbid a Christian youth to love money and worldly honor, since these evils are also condemned among the heathen? No one who will serve covetousness will become a Christian, for this vice has not only ruined individual characters, but also well-fortified cities and powerful kingdoms. Covetousness will overthrow any government that comes under its sway. When this vice has taken possession of the mind, no good influence can affect it. Covetousness is a deadly poison and yet, sad to say, it has spread and has become very powerful among us. Only through Christ can we destroy this vice within ourselves, and we can do it if we very diligently and unceasingly follow Him; for what did He oppose more than this root of all evil?

The learning of chivalrous arts [*ritterlicher Kuenste*—Moerikofer] I do not condemn so strongly; but if I did not see that some rich youths even shun exercise and manual labor, through which much good would accrue to common life, I should judge otherwise [i. e., should prefer manual labor to these arts.—Fulda's Notes.]. It behooves a Christian, however, in so far as the common good and the peace of all will allow it, not to take up arms at all. Although David was not trained to use arms, yet the Lord God caused him to triumph over Goliath with a sling and He protected the unarmed Israelites from the overwhelming power of their enemies. In the same manner He will doubtless also help and protect us; but if it should please Him to do otherwise, He would arm our hands and train them for the conflict. If a youth, however, desires to become skillful in handling arms, let his only object be to prepare himself to fight for his country and to shield those whom God calls upon him to protect.

I would that all men, and particularly those who are set apart to preach the Gospel, felt as if they ought to live nowhere else except in the ancient city of Massilia, in which no one was received for citizenship, who had no trade which would enable him to make a living. Wherever we would carry out this thought, idleness, which is a fruitful source of all wantonness, would be driven away; and our bodies would become much healthier, stronger, and better fitted to endure hardships.[4]

PART III.

How A Youth Should Act
Towards Other Persons

A free and noble youth should reflect on his duties to others, in the following manner: Christ suffered death in my stead and became my Savior; therefore I should offer my services to the good of all men, and I must not suppose that I belong to myself but to my neighbor. I was not born in order that I should live for myself, but in order that I might become all things to all men.

Every young man should, from early youth, strive after steadiness, faithfulness, truth, faith, righteousness, and piety; and he should diligently practice these things. With these he can serve, with fruitful results, the cause of Christianity, society around him, and his country; for he will be useful to the body politic as well as to the individual citizen. Those are weak-minded persons who are concerned only about living a quiet life. They are not so godlike as those who, to their own detriment, diligently serve all men.

We ought to be very careful, at the same time, that those things which we undertake to the glory of God, to the honor of our country, and for the common welfare be not defiled by self and Satan, so that we do not, at last, turn to our own advantage what we wish to be regarded as having been done for the good of others. There are many who begin well and go in the right direction, but they soon become corrupted by vain ambition, which poisons and destroys every good resolution, and as a result they are led away from all that is good and noble.

One who is a Christian will look upon the fortune or misfortune of others as if either one had happened to himself. If another person is fortunate, the Christian will rejoice as if good fortune had befallen himself; on the other hand, he will be sad when misfortune falls to the lot of another. The Christian will regard a community as a household, yea, as one body in which all members enjoy pleasure or suffer pain. Such members will so assist one another that what happens to one will be regarded as happening to all. For this reason the Christian will rejoice with them that rejoice and weep with them that weep. Any event in the life of another he will regard as occurring in his own life; for, as Seneca says, what happens to one person may happen to any other person.

A Christian youth should not so manifest joy or sadness as the common custom is, however; that is to say, he should not become proud and vain in prosperity, nor should he become impatient and finally despair in adversity. Inasmuch as a Christian will not be able to pass through life without these and other temptations and trials, he will, if he be wise, so deliberately and discreetly control them that he will at no time and in no place deviate from that which is becoming and right. He will thus be as glad when others are prosperous, as when he is prosperous; but he will not give way to despair when reverses come. In other words, he will endure all things calmly and with moderation.

I am not in favor of forbidding a youth to join the company of men and women assembled for innocent pleasure in public places. I refer to weddings of relatives, annual celebrations and festivals; for I learn that even Christ did not refuse to be present at a wedding. Since people will have festive occasions, I very much prefer that they be held openly, instead of secretly or in suspicious homes. Some persons are so constituted that they are afraid to act in a crowd. They are very easily frightened, when a person who may bear testimony against them sees them act; but when they act in secret, the accusing voice of conscience can scarcely frighten them. One must be a desperate rogue, a man from whom no good can be expected, if he is not ashamed to act dishonorably in the presence of a public audience.

Where persons assemble in social gatherings, every youth attending them should see to it that he go away morally benefited; so that he may not, as Socrates complains, always come home morally worse than he was before. He should therefore be watchful and diligent to follow the example of those who conduct themselves honorably and uprightly on social occasions; but, on the other hand, when he observes persons behaving themselves unbecomingly or shamefully, let him beware of imitating them.

Those, however, who are grown up and have become bold and fixed in their habits are hardly able to restrain themselves in this manner; therefore my advice is, that the youth should attend public gatherings, for social purposes, all the more rarely. Should a youth perchance be led into the folly of others, he ought by all means to turn away from it and should come to himself at the earliest moment. His reason for thus withdrawing from such association will satisfy those persons who know that his desire is, always to be intent on doing what is noblest and best.

When a neighbor is in trouble, we should at once visit him. In such cases it is, indeed, becoming for us to be first to go to his rescue and last to leave him. We should exert ourselves manfully in his behalf, by investigating the harm done, by doing something to remove hindrances, and by rendering any other assistance or giving advice.

Next to God we should honor and highly esteem our parents. This practice is also prevalent among the heathen as well as among unbelievers. Our will should yield to that of our parents, everywhere ;and if they sometimes do not live up to the commands of our Savior, we, as believers in Christ, should not rashly oppose them ; but we should rather explain to them, very kindly, what one ought to do or say. Should they be unwilling to accept such explanations, we ought to let them go rather than insult them with reproach or derision.

Anger, as physicians say, comes from a hasty temper. Since the young are very passionate, every youth should diligently refrain from becoming angry, so that he will neither say nor do anything that is prompted by anger. While anger lasts, let everything that comes to the mind be looked upon with suspicion.

If, at any time, we cannot accept and bear injustice or insults heaped upon us, because it seems to us too much to be endured, we should bring the matter before the magistrate or any other proper government officer. To return a reproachful remark for an insult or to abuse again, when we are abused, is nothing else than to become like him whom we thus treat.

Games played with one's companions, at proper times, I allow, provided they are games that require skill and serve to train the body. Games with numbers require skill, as they involve a knowledge of arithmetic. Games requiring movement, such as chess, also require skill; since one must carefully plan when and where to move, and when not to move. Chess, more than all other games, teaches the player not to take a single step without forethought. It is necessary, however, in playing this game to know when to quit; for some persons have been found, who neglected useful and serious occupations, in order to give their time and talents to playing chess. Only occasionally and, as it were, in passing by, would I allow such games. Cards and dice I reject entirely and would consign them to the carrion-pit.

The plays and games which exercise the body are running, jumping, stone throwing or putting the shot, wrestling, and the like. Nearly all nations engage in them; and among our Swiss ancestors they have been very popular, and they may be regarded as very useful for some purposes. Wrestling is an exercise in which the youth should engage very cautiously and not too often; for some have made earnest of the exercise and have turned it into a fight. I have not yet seen much benefit derived from swimming, although it is sometimes good sport to stretch out one's limbs in the water and to move like a fish. Swimming has been useful, it is true, in a few cases. As examples I may mention the one who swam from the Capitol and announced to Camillus the miserable condition of the avaricious city of Rome. Cloelia also swam back to her friends at Rome.[5]

All our walk and conversation should be such that those with whom we live will be benefited thereby. If it be necessary at any time to reprove or punish any one, let it be done so pleasantly, so thoughtfully, so skillfully, and with such judgment that we shall be enabled to drive away the evil, and shall win back the person and draw him more closely to ourselves.

We ought to be so diligent and firm in standing by the truth, that we not only weigh our own words but also the words of all other persons, in such a manner that no deception, no lie can be concealed therein. A candid mind should never be more displeased with itself than it is, when it finds itself giving utterance to a lie, even under oppression and therefore unwillingly; and I need not say that a youth should be not a little frightened and ashamed, were he to observe that he willfully gives utterance to light, untruthful language, whether such language be imitated from other persons or whether it be his own invention. A man who is a Christian is commanded to speak the truth to his neighbor; therefore one who is a Christian should stand firmly by the truth. A double-minded man is unstable in all his ways. He who does not stand by his word or is untruthful, is not to be trusted. The words uttered by the mouth intimate what is in the heart. If the words are frivolous and deceitful we have a sure sign that the heart is worse than the words. Such a person may conceal his deceitfulness for a short time, but it will be discovered by and by. How foolish is the man who knows very well that he lies, but imagines that he is so much better than he really is, because no one else knows that he is a liar!

Men ought to be truthful not only in words but also in all their actions, never pretending to be what they are not, nor falsely representing anything in their dealings. As the heart, the spring of action is, so should the countenance, the eyes, and all one's manner be. He who feigns the gait of another thereby discloses the fact that his step does not correspond to his character; in other words, that his heart is unchaste and frivolous.

What more shall I say? Let every youth diligently see to it that he drinks from the clear and pure fountain of life, which is the Lord Jesus Christ. He who does this will be shown by Christ how to live, how to speak, and how to act. He will no more regard himself above exercising piety and doing right; he will never despair. He will grow in grace daily; nevertheless he will observe that he often fails and falters. In this way he will make rapid progress, but he will still count himself among the most unworthy. He will do good to all men and will revile no one; for thus did Christ set an example. Hence, he will be perfect who undertakes diligently to follow Christ only.

Conclusion

These things, my dear Gerald, I have regarded as helpful to instruct and train good and noble youth; although my thoughts, as everyone can plainly see, are very much disconnected and lack methodical arrangement.

Let your own mind, however, dwell on these things. Carry out and improve, in your manner of living, what I have here outlined and roughly worked out. If you do this, you will, indeed, beautifully weave into your own life what I have here written without good order, and you will thus be a living example of the model which I have herein placed before you. Yes, I dare say that, if you practice these things, you cannot fail to become much more refined, cultured, and more nearly perfect than I have been able to outline for you.

It will be necessary, however, for you to go to work vigorously and to strain every nerve. This will help you very much to drive away indolence, the mother of all vice; for many persons, having formed habits of laziness, in early youth, soon become so shamefully indolent that they loiter about, as if they purposely wanted to be devourers of other persons' goods, or even cesspools of all vices. You, on the other hand, devote the spring-time of your life to that which is good and useful, because time passes rapidly and better opportunities seldom present themselves in later years. No time of life is more promising for doing good than youth. Not the man who can only talk much about God is a Christian, but he who labors faithfully with God to do great and holy things; therefore, my pious and noble youth, continue to lift up and adorn your noble family, your handsome person, and your patrimony— all advantages that you enjoy—with these true ornaments.

I have said less than I ought to say. Regard nothing as a true ornament but virtue, piety, and honor. Nobility, beauty, and riches are not intrinsic good, but they are conditioned by good fortune.[6]

May God preserve you blameless by his grace, so that you may never be separated from Him. Amen.

Notes

Words in brackets are inserted by the translator to explain the text or to quote authorities.

1. The gymnasium was really only an important part of the Carolinum. The sick were also visited and other pastoral duties were performed.

2. Fulda's opinion is that Zwingli did not intend to contrast the Latin with the Greek scholars, but the Vulgate with the original text.

3. Zwingli, in his peculiar way, strikes at a leading cause of dyspepsia, with its train of physical, social, and moral disorders. Epicures still exist, even among professing Christians. How sinful it is to boast of how much of a dainty dish one can eat! Ecclesiasticus 37: 29-31.

4. Massilia, now Marseilles, as a Greek colony had strict laws. Valerius Maximus II., 6, hints at Zwingli's thought.—*Fulda.*

5. The one who swam from the Capitol was Pontius Cominius, as Plutarch says in volume one, page 115. A reference to Smith's Classical Dictionary, page 214, will show that Zwingli was correct in regard to Cloelia's act.

6. Gerald Meyer descended from a noble family and Zwingli was concerned in preserving him from the corrupt habits of the nobility of that time, by teaching him how to be noble at heart.

Also from Gideon House Books

Sovereign Grace by D.L. Moody

God's Light in Dark Clouds by Theodore Cuyler

A Church in the House by Matthew Henry

Indwelling Sin in Believers by John Owen

Secret Power by D.L. Moody

Thoughts for Young Men by J.C. Ryle

The Divine Liturgy of St. John Chrysostom

A Study on Dispensationalism by A.W. Pink

Prevailing Prayer: What Hinders It by D.L. Moody

The Duty of Pastors by John Owen

The Expulsive Power of a New Affection by Thomas Chalmers

According to Promise by Charles Spurgeon

The Resurrection: A Symposium by Charles Spurgeon

The Acceptable Sacrifice by John Bunyan

Find these titles and more at
www.gideonhousebooks.com

www.ingramcontent.com/pod-product-compliance
Lightning Source LLC
Chambersburg PA
CBHW060043040426
42331CB00032B/2256